Podcas

INFORMATIONS

NAME

ADDRESS

E-MAIL ADDRESS

WEBSITE

PHONE   FAX

EMERGENCY CONTACT PERSON

PHONE   FAX

Podcast name

....

EPISODE #

RECORDING DATE

PUBLISHING DATE

RECORDING LOCATION

TOPIC TO DISCUSS

....
....
....
....
....
....

HOSTS	GUESTS	LENGTH

MAIN GOAL FOR THIS PODCAST

....
....
....
....

CONTEST

SPONSOR ....
PRIZE ....
WINNER ....

TALKING POINTS

....
....
....
....
....
....

Podcast Review

THINGS I NEED TO PRACTICE

THINGS I REALLY ENJOYED :)

THINGS I DIDN'T EXPECTED

BUSINESS / PROMOTION

NOTES

Podcast Rating ☆ ☆ ☆ ☆ ☆

Podcast name

EPISODE #

RECORDING DATE

PUBLISHING DATE

RECORDING LOCATION

TOPIC TO DISCUSS

HOSTS	GUESTS	LENGTH

MAIN GOAL FOR THIS PODCAST

CONTEST

SPONSOR

PRIZE

WINNER

TALKING POINTS

Podcast Review

THINGS I NEED TO PRACTICE

....
....
....
....

THINGS I REALLY ENJOYED :)

....
....
....
....

THINGS I DIDN'T EXPECTED

....
....
....
....

BUSINESS / PROMOTION

....
....
....
....
....
....

NOTES

....
....
....
....
....
....

Podcast Rating ⭐ ⭐ ⭐ ⭐ ⭐

Podcast name

....

EPISODE #

RECORDING DATE

PUBLISHING DATE

RECORDING LOCATION

TOPIC TO DISCUSS

....
....
....
....
....
....
....

HOSTS	GUESTS	LENGTH

MAIN GOAL FOR THIS PODCAST

....
....
....
....

CONTEST

SPONSOR ....
PRIZE ....
WINNER ....

TALKING POINTS

....
....
....
....
....
....

Podcast Review

THINGS I NEED TO PRACTICE

....
....
....
....

THINGS I REALLY ENJOYED :)

....
....
....
....

THINGS I DIDN'T EXPECTED

....
....
....
....

BUSINESS / PROMOTION

....
....
....
....
....

NOTES

....
....
....
....
....

Podcast Rating

Podcast name

EPISODE

RECORDING DATE

PUBLISHING DATE

RECORDING LOCATION

TOPIC TO DISCUSS

HOSTS

GUESTS

LENGTH

MAIN GOAL FOR THIS PODCAST

CONTEST

SPONSOR

PRIZE

WINNER

TALKING POINTS

Podcast Review

THINGS I NEED TO PRACTICE

....
....
....
....

THINGS I REALLY ENJOYED :)

....
....
....
....

THINGS I DIDN'T EXPECTED

....
....
....

BUSINESS / PROMOTION

....
....
....
....
....

NOTES

....
....
....
....
....

Podcast Rating

Podcast name

....

EPISODE #

RECORDING DATE

PUBLISHING DATE

RECORDING LOCATION

TOPIC TO DISCUSS

....
....
....
....
....
....
....

HOSTS

GUESTS

LENGTH

MAIN GOAL FOR THIS PODCAST

....
....
....
....

CONTEST

SPONSOR ....
PRIZE ....
WINNER ....

TALKING POINTS

....
....
....
....
....
....

Podcast Review

THINGS I NEED TO PRACTICE

....

....

....

....

THINGS I REALLY ENJOYED :)

....

....

....

....

THINGS I DIDN'T EXPECTED

....

....

....

....

BUSINESS / PROMOTION

....

....

....

....

....

NOTES

....

....

....

....

....

Podcast Rating ☆ ☆ ☆ ☆ ☆

Podcast name

....

EPISODE

RECORDING DATE

PUBLISHING DATE

RECORDING LOCATION

TOPIC TO DISCUSS

....
....
....
....
....
....
....

HOSTS

GUESTS

LENGTH

MAIN GOAL FOR THIS PODCAST

....
....
....
....

CONTEST

SPONSOR ....
PRIZE ....
WINNER ....

TALKING POINTS

....
....
....
....
....
....

Podcast Review

THINGS I NEED TO PRACTICE

....
....
....
....

THINGS I REALLY ENJOYED :)

....
....
....
....

THINGS I DIDN'T EXPECTED

....
....
....
....

BUSINESS / PROMOTION

....
....
....
....
....

NOTES

....
....
....
....
....

Podcast Rating

Podcast name

....

EPISODE #

RECORDING DATE

PUBLISHING DATE

RECORDING LOCATION

TOPIC TO DISCUSS

....
....
....
....
....
....
....

HOSTS	GUESTS	LENGTH

MAIN GOAL FOR THIS PODCAST

....
....
....
....

CONTEST

SPONSOR ....
PRIZE ....
WINNER ....

TALKING POINTS

....
....
....
....
....
....

Podcast Review

THINGS I NEED TO PRACTICE

THINGS I REALLY ENJOYED :)

THINGS I DIDN'T EXPECTED

BUSINESS / PROMOTION

NOTES

Podcast Rating

Podcast name

....

EPISODE #

RECORDING DATE

PUBLISHING DATE

RECORDING LOCATION

TOPIC TO DISCUSS

....
....
....
....
....
....
....

HOSTS

GUESTS

LENGTH

MAIN GOAL FOR THIS PODCAST

....
....
....
....

CONTEST

SPONSOR ....
PRIZE ....
WINNER ....

TALKING POINTS

....
....
....
....
....
....

Podcast Review

THINGS I NEED TO PRACTICE

....
....
....
....

THINGS I REALLY ENJOYED :)

....
....
....
....

THINGS I DIDN'T EXPECTED

....
....
....
....

BUSINESS / PROMOTION

....
....
....
....
....

NOTES

....
....
....
....
....

Podcast Rating

Podcast name

EPISODE

RECORDING DATE

PUBLISHING DATE

RECORDING LOCATION

TOPIC TO DISCUSS

HOSTS

GUESTS

LENGTH

MAIN GOAL FOR THIS PODCAST

CONTEST

SPONSOR

PRIZE

WINNER

TALKING POINTS

Podcast Review

THINGS I NEED TO PRACTICE

THINGS I REALLY ENJOYED :)

THINGS I DIDN'T EXPECTED

BUSINESS / PROMOTION

NOTES

Podcast Rating

Podcast name

....

EPISODE #

RECORDING DATE

PUBLISHING DATE

RECORDING LOCATION

TOPIC TO DISCUSS

....
....
....
....
....
....
....

HOSTS

GUESTS

LENGTH

MAIN GOAL FOR THIS PODCAST

....
....
....
....

CONTEST

SPONSOR ....
PRIZE ....
WINNER ....

TALKING POINTS

....
....
....
....
....
....

Podcast Review

THINGS I REALLY ENJOYED :)

THINGS I DIDN'T EXPECTED

BUSINESS / PROMOTION

NOTES

Podcast Rating

Podcast name

....

EPISODE

RECORDING DATE

PUBLISHING DATE

RECORDING LOCATION

TOPIC TO DISCUSS

....
....
....
....
....
....
....

HOSTS

GUESTS

LENGTH

MAIN GOAL FOR THIS PODCAST

....
....
....
....

CONTEST

SPONSOR ....

PRIZE ....

WINNER ....

TALKING POINTS

....
....
....
....
....
....

Podcast Review

THINGS I NEED TO PRACTICE

THINGS I REALLY ENJOYED :)

THINGS I DIDN'T EXPECTED

BUSINESS / PROMOTION

NOTES

Podcast Rating ⭐ ⭐ ⭐ ⭐ ⭐

Podcast name

....

EPISODE #

RECORDING DATE

PUBLISHING DATE

RECORDING LOCATION

TOPIC TO DISCUSS

....
....
....
....
....
....

HOSTS	GUESTS	LENGTH

MAIN GOAL FOR THIS PODCAST

....
....
....
....

CONTEST

SPONSOR ....
PRIZE ....
WINNER ....

TALKING POINTS

....
....
....
....
....
....

Podcast Review

THINGS I NEED TO PRACTICE

....
....
....
....

THINGS I REALLY ENJOYED :)

....
....
....
....

THINGS I DIDN'T EXPECTED

....
....
....
....

BUSINESS / PROMOTION

....
....
....
....
....

NOTES

....
....
....
....
....

Podcast Rating ☆ ☆ ☆ ☆ ☆

Podcast name

....

EPISODE #

RECORDING DATE

PUBLISHING DATE

RECORDING LOCATION

TOPIC TO DISCUSS

....
....
....
....
....
....
....

HOSTS

GUESTS

LENGTH

MAIN GOAL FOR THIS PODCAST

....
....
....
....

CONTEST

SPONSOR ....
PRIZE ....
WINNER ....

TALKING POINTS

....
....
....
....
....
....

Podcast Review

THINGS I NEED TO PRACTICE

....
....
....
....

THINGS I REALLY ENJOYED :)

....
....
....
....

THINGS I DIDN'T EXPECTED

....
....
....
....

BUSINESS / PROMOTION

....
....
....
....
....

NOTES

....
....
....
....
....
....

Podcast Rating

Podcast name

....

EPISODE

RECORDING DATE

PUBLISHING DATE

RECORDING LOCATION

TOPIC TO DISCUSS

....
....
....
....
....
....
....

HOSTS

GUESTS

LENGTH

MAIN GOAL FOR THIS PODCAST

....
....
....
....

CONTEST

SPONSOR ....
PRIZE ....
WINNER ....

TALKING POINTS

....
....
....
....
....
....

Podcast Review

THINGS I NEED TO PRACTICE

....
....
....
....

THINGS I REALLY ENJOYED :)

....
....
....
....

THINGS I DIDN'T EXPECTED

....
....
....
....

BUSINESS / PROMOTION

....
....
....
....
....

NOTES

....
....
....
....
....

Podcast Rating ⭐ ⭐ ⭐ ⭐ ⭐

Podcast name

EPISODE

RECORDING DATE

PUBLISHING DATE

RECORDING LOCATION

TOPIC TO DISCUSS

HOSTS

GUESTS

LENGTH

MAIN GOAL FOR THIS PODCAST

CONTEST

SPONSOR

PRIZE

WINNER

TALKING POINTS

Podcast Review

THINGS I NEED TO PRACTICE

....
....
....
....

THINGS I REALLY ENJOYED :)

....
....
....
....

THINGS I DIDN'T EXPECTED

....
....
....

BUSINESS / PROMOTION

....
....
....
....
....

NOTES

....
....
....
....
....

Podcast Rating

Podcast name

....

EPISODE #

RECORDING DATE

PUBLISHING DATE

RECORDING LOCATION

TOPIC TO DISCUSS

....
....
....
....
....
....
....

HOSTS	GUESTS	LENGTH

MAIN GOAL FOR THIS PODCAST

....
....
....
....

CONTEST

SPONSOR ....
PRIZE ....
WINNER ....

TALKING POINTS

....
....
....
....
....
....

Podcast Review

THINGS I NEED TO PRACTICE

....
....
....
....

THINGS I REALLY ENJOYED :)

....
....
....
....

THINGS I DIDN'T EXPECTED

....
....
....
....

BUSINESS / PROMOTION

....
....
....
....
....

NOTES

....
....
....
....
....

Podcast Rating

Podcast name

....

EPISODE #

RECORDING DATE

PUBLISHING DATE

RECORDING LOCATION

TOPIC TO DISCUSS

....
....
....
....
....
....
....

HOSTS	GUESTS	LENGTH

MAIN GOAL FOR THIS PODCAST

....
....
....
....

CONTEST

SPONSOR ....

PRIZE ....

WINNER ....

TALKING POINTS

....
....
....
....
....
....

Podcast Review

THINGS I NEED TO PRACTICE

....
....
....
....

THINGS I REALLY ENJOYED :)

....
....
....
....

THINGS I DIDN'T EXPECTED

....
....
....

BUSINESS / PROMOTION

....
....
....
....
....

NOTES

....
....
....
....
....

Podcast Rating

Podcast name

....

EPISODE #

RECORDING DATE

PUBLISHING DATE

RECORDING LOCATION

TOPIC TO DISCUSS

....
....
....
....
....
....
....

HOSTS	GUESTS	LENGTH

MAIN GOAL FOR THIS PODCAST

....
....
....
....

CONTEST

SPONSOR ....
PRIZE ....
WINNER ....

TALKING POINTS

....
....
....
....
....
....

Podcast Review

THINGS I NEED TO PRACTICE

....
....
....
....

THINGS I REALLY ENJOYED :)

....
....
....
....

THINGS I DIDN'T EXPECTED

....
....
....
....

BUSINESS / PROMOTION

....
....
....
....
....
....

NOTES

....
....
....
....
....

Podcast Rating

Podcast name

....

EPISODE #

RECORDING DATE

PUBLISHING DATE

RECORDING LOCATION

TOPIC TO DISCUSS

....
....
....
....
....
....
....

HOSTS

GUESTS

LENGTH

MAIN GOAL FOR THIS PODCAST

....
....
....
....

CONTEST

SPONSOR ....
PRIZE ....
WINNER ....

TALKING POINTS

....
....
....
....
....
....

Podcast Review

THINGS I NEED TO PRACTICE

THINGS I REALLY ENJOYED :)

THINGS I DIDN'T EXPECTED

BUSINESS / PROMOTION

NOTES

Podcast Rating

Podcast name

EPISODE #

RECORDING DATE

PUBLISHING DATE

RECORDING LOCATION

TOPIC TO DISCUSS

HOSTS

GUESTS

LENGTH

MAIN GOAL FOR THIS PODCAST

CONTEST

SPONSOR
PRIZE
WINNER

TALKING POINTS

Podcast Review

THINGS I NEED TO PRACTICE

....
....
....
....

THINGS I REALLY ENJOYED :)

....
....
....
....

THINGS I DIDN'T EXPECTED

....
....
....
....

BUSINESS / PROMOTION

....
....
....
....
....

NOTES

....
....
....
....
....

Podcast Rating

Podcast name

....

EPISODE #

RECORDING DATE

PUBLISHING DATE

RECORDING LOCATION

TOPIC TO DISCUSS

....
....
....
....
....
....
....

HOSTS

GUESTS

LENGTH

MAIN GOAL FOR THIS PODCAST

....
....
....
....

CONTEST

SPONSOR ....
PRIZE ....
WINNER ....

TALKING POINTS

....
....
....
....
....
....
....

Podcast Review

THINGS I NEED TO PRACTICE

....
....
....
....

THINGS I REALLY ENJOYED :)

....
....
....
....

THINGS I DIDN'T EXPECTED

....
....
....
....

BUSINESS / PROMOTION

....
....
....
....
....
....

NOTES

....
....
....
....
....
....

Podcast Rating

Podcast name

....

EPISODE #

RECORDING DATE

PUBLISHING DATE

RECORDING LOCATION

TOPIC TO DISCUSS

....
....
....
....
....
....
....

HOSTS	GUESTS	LENGTH

MAIN GOAL FOR THIS PODCAST

....
....
....
....

CONTEST

SPONSOR ....
PRIZE ....
WINNER ....

TALKING POINTS

....
....
....
....
....
....

Podcast Review

THINGS I NEED TO PRACTICE

THINGS I REALLY ENJOYED :)

THINGS I DIDN'T EXPECTED

BUSINESS / PROMOTION

NOTES

Podcast Rating

Podcast name

....

EPISODE #

RECORDING DATE

PUBLISHING DATE

RECORDING LOCATION

TOPIC TO DISCUSS

....
....
....
....
....
....
....

HOSTS

GUESTS

LENGTH

MAIN GOAL FOR THIS PODCAST

....
....
....
....

CONTEST

SPONSOR ....
PRIZE ....
WINNER ....

TALKING POINTS

....
....
....
....
....
....

Podcast Review

THINGS I NEED TO PRACTICE

....
....
....
....

THINGS I REALLY ENJOYED :)

....
....
....
....

THINGS I DIDN'T EXPECTED

....
....
....
....

BUSINESS / PROMOTION

....
....
....
....
....

NOTES

....
....
....
....
....

Podcast Rating

Podcast name

....

EPISODE #

RECORDING DATE

PUBLISHING DATE

RECORDING LOCATION

TOPIC TO DISCUSS

....
....
....
....
....
....
....

HOSTS

GUESTS

LENGTH

MAIN GOAL FOR THIS PODCAST

....
....
....
....

CONTEST

SPONSOR ....
PRIZE ....
WINNER ....

TALKING POINTS

....
....
....
....
....
....

Podcast Review

THINGS I NEED TO PRACTICE

....
....
....
....

THINGS I REALLY ENJOYED :)

....
....
....
....

THINGS I DIDN'T EXPECTED

....
....
....
....

BUSINESS / PROMOTION

....
....
....
....
....
....

NOTES

....
....
....
....
....
....

Podcast Rating ☆ ☆ ☆ ☆ ☆

Podcast name

....

EPISODE #

RECORDING DATE

PUBLISHING DATE

RECORDING LOCATION

TOPIC TO DISCUSS

....
....
....
....
....
....
....

HOSTS	GUESTS	LENGTH

MAIN GOAL FOR THIS PODCAST

....
....
....
....

CONTEST

SPONSOR ....
PRIZE ....
WINNER ....

TALKING POINTS

....
....
....
....
....
....

Podcast Review

THINGS I NEED TO PRACTICE

....
....
....
....

THINGS I REALLY ENJOYED :)

....
....
....
....

THINGS I DIDN'T EXPECTED

....
....
....
....

BUSINESS / PROMOTION

....
....
....
....

NOTES

....
....
....
....
....

Podcast Rating ⭐ ⭐ ⭐ ⭐ ⭐

Podcast name

....

EPISODE #

RECORDING DATE

PUBLISHING DATE

RECORDING LOCATION

TOPIC TO DISCUSS

....
....
....
....
....
....
....

HOSTS	GUESTS	LENGTH

MAIN GOAL FOR THIS PODCAST

....
....
....
....

CONTEST

SPONSOR ....
PRIZE ....
WINNER ....

TALKING POINTS

....
....
....
....
....
....

Podcast Review

THINGS I NEED TO PRACTICE

....
....
....
....

THINGS I REALLY ENJOYED :)

....
....
....
....

THINGS I DIDN'T EXPECTED

....
....
....
....

BUSINESS / PROMOTION

....
....
....
....
....

NOTES

....
....
....
....
....

Podcast Rating

Podcast name

....

EPISODE #

RECORDING DATE

PUBLISHING DATE

RECORDING LOCATION

TOPIC TO DISCUSS

....
....
....
....
....
....
....

HOSTS

GUESTS

LENGTH

MAIN GOAL FOR THIS PODCAST

....
....
....
....

CONTEST

SPONSOR ....
PRIZE ....
WINNER ....

TALKING POINTS

....
....
....
....
....
....

Podcast Review

THINGS I NEED TO PRACTICE

THINGS I REALLY ENJOYED :)

THINGS I DIDN'T EXPECTED

BUSINESS / PROMOTION

NOTES

Podcast Rating

Podcast name

....

EPISODE #

RECORDING DATE

PUBLISHING DATE

RECORDING LOCATION

TOPIC TO DISCUSS

....
....
....
....
....
....
....

HOSTS

GUESTS

LENGTH

MAIN GOAL FOR THIS PODCAST

....
....
....
....

CONTEST

SPONSOR ....
PRIZE ....
WINNER ....

TALKING POINTS

....
....
....
....
....
....

Podcast Review

THINGS I NEED TO PRACTICE

....
....
....
....

THINGS I REALLY ENJOYED :)

....
....
....
....

THINGS I DIDN'T EXPECTED

....
....
....
....

BUSINESS / PROMOTION

....
....
....
....
....
....

NOTES

....
....
....
....
....

Podcast Rating

Podcast name

EPISODE

RECORDING DATE

PUBLISHING DATE

RECORDING LOCATION

TOPIC TO DISCUSS

HOSTS

GUESTS

LENGTH

MAIN GOAL FOR THIS PODCAST

CONTEST

SPONSOR
PRIZE
WINNER

TALKING POINTS

Podcast Review

THINGS I NEED TO PRACTICE

....
....
....
....

THINGS I REALLY ENJOYED :)

....
....
....
....

THINGS I DIDN'T EXPECTED

....
....
....
....

BUSINESS / PROMOTION

....
....
....
....
....

NOTES

....
....
....
....
....

Podcast Rating

Podcast name

....

EPISODE

RECORDING DATE

PUBLISHING DATE

RECORDING LOCATION

TOPIC TO DISCUSS

....
....
....
....
....
....
....

HOSTS

GUESTS

LENGTH

MAIN GOAL FOR THIS PODCAST

....
....
....
....

CONTEST

SPONSOR ....
PRIZE ....
WINNER ....

TALKING POINTS

....
....
....
....
....

Podcast Review

THINGS I NEED TO PRACTICE

....
....
....
....

THINGS I REALLY ENJOYED :)

....
....
....
....

THINGS I DIDN'T EXPECTED

....
....
....
....

BUSINESS / PROMOTION

....
....
....
....
....
....

NOTES

....
....
....
....
....
....

Podcast Rating

Podcast name

....

EPISODE

RECORDING DATE

PUBLISHING DATE

RECORDING LOCATION

TOPIC TO DISCUSS

....
....
....
....
....
....
....

HOSTS

GUESTS

LENGTH

MAIN GOAL FOR THIS PODCAST

....
....
....
....

CONTEST

SPONSOR ....
PRIZE ....
WINNER ....

TALKING POINTS

....
....
....
....
....
....

Podcast Review

THINGS I NEED TO PRACTICE

....
....
....
....

THINGS I REALLY ENJOYED :)

....
....
....
....

THINGS I DIDN'T EXPECTED

....
....
....
....

BUSINESS / PROMOTION

....
....
....
....
....
....

NOTES

....
....
....
....
....
....

Podcast Rating

Podcast name

....

EPISODE

RECORDING DATE

PUBLISHING DATE

RECORDING LOCATION

TOPIC TO DISCUSS

....
....
....
....
....
....
....

HOSTS

GUESTS

LENGTH

MAIN GOAL FOR THIS PODCAST

....
....
....
....

CONTEST

SPONSOR ....
PRIZE ....
WINNER ....

TALKING POINTS

....
....
....
....
....
....

Podcast Review

THINGS I NEED TO PRACTICE

....
....
....
....

THINGS I REALLY ENJOYED :)

....
....
....
....

THINGS I DIDN'T EXPECTED

....
....
....
....

BUSINESS / PROMOTION

....
....
....
....
....

NOTES

....
....
....
....
....
....

Podcast Rating

Podcast name

....

EPISODE #

RECORDING DATE

PUBLISHING DATE

RECORDING LOCATION

TOPIC TO DISCUSS

....
....
....
....
....
....
....

HOSTS	GUESTS	LENGTH

MAIN GOAL FOR THIS PODCAST

....
....
....
....

CONTEST

SPONSOR ....
PRIZE ....
WINNER ....

TALKING POINTS

....
....
....
....
....
....

Podcast Review

THINGS I NEED TO PRACTICE

....
....
....
....

THINGS I REALLY ENJOYED :)

....
....
....
....

THINGS I DIDN'T EXPECTED

....
....
....
....

BUSINESS / PROMOTION

....
....
....
....
....
....

NOTES

....
....
....
....
....

Podcast Rating

Podcast name

....

EPISODE #

RECORDING DATE

PUBLISHING DATE

RECORDING LOCATION

TOPIC TO DISCUSS

....
....
....
....
....
....
....

HOSTS	GUESTS	LENGTH

MAIN GOAL FOR THIS PODCAST

....
....
....
....

CONTEST

SPONSOR ....

PRIZE ....

WINNER ....

TALKING POINTS

....
....
....
....
....
....

Podcast Review

THINGS I NEED TO PRACTICE

....
....
....
....

THINGS I REALLY ENJOYED :)

....
....
....
....

THINGS I DIDN'T EXPECTED

....
....
....
....

BUSINESS / PROMOTION

....
....
....
....
....

NOTES

....
....
....
....
....
....

Podcast Rating

Podcast name

....

EPISODE #

RECORDING DATE

PUBLISHING DATE

RECORDING LOCATION

TOPIC TO DISCUSS

....
....
....
....
....
....
....

HOSTS	GUESTS	LENGTH

MAIN GOAL FOR THIS PODCAST

....
....
....
....

CONTEST

SPONSOR ....
PRIZE ....
WINNER ....

TALKING POINTS

....
....
....
....
....
....

Podcast Review

THINGS I NEED TO PRACTICE

....
....
....
....

THINGS I REALLY ENJOYED :)

....
....
....
....

THINGS I DIDN'T EXPECTED

....
....
....
....

BUSINESS / PROMOTION

....
....
....
....
....

NOTES

....
....
....
....
....
....

Podcast Rating

Podcast name

....

EPISODE #

RECORDING DATE

PUBLISHING DATE

RECORDING LOCATION

TOPIC TO DISCUSS

....
....
....
....
....
....
....

HOSTS

GUESTS

LENGTH

MAIN GOAL FOR THIS PODCAST

....
....
....
....

CONTEST

SPONSOR ....
PRIZE ....
WINNER ....

TALKING POINTS

....
....
....
....
....
....

Podcast Review

THINGS I NEED TO PRACTICE

....
....
....
....

THINGS I REALLY ENJOYED :)

....
....
....
....

THINGS I DIDN'T EXPECTED

....
....
....
....

BUSINESS / PROMOTION

....
....
....
....
....

NOTES

....
....
....
....
....

Podcast Rating

Podcast name

....

EPISODE #

RECORDING DATE

PUBLISHING DATE

RECORDING LOCATION

TOPIC TO DISCUSS

....
....
....
....
....
....
....

HOSTS

GUESTS

LENGTH

MAIN GOAL FOR THIS PODCAST

....
....
....
....

CONTEST

SPONSOR ....
PRIZE ....
WINNER ....

TALKING POINTS

....
....
....
....
....
....

Podcast Review

THINGS I NEED TO PRACTICE

THINGS I REALLY ENJOYED :)

THINGS I DIDN'T EXPECTED

BUSINESS / PROMOTION

NOTES

Podcast Rating

Podcast name ....

EPISODE #

RECORDING DATE

PUBLISHING DATE

RECORDING LOCATION

TOPIC TO DISCUSS

....
....
....
....
....
....
....

HOSTS

GUESTS

LENGTH

MAIN GOAL FOR THIS PODCAST

....
....
....
....

CONTEST

SPONSOR ....
PRIZE ....
WINNER ....

TALKING POINTS

....
....
....
....
....
....

Podcast Review

THINGS I NEED TO PRACTICE

THINGS I REALLY ENJOYED :)

THINGS I DIDN'T EXPECTED

BUSINESS / PROMOTION

NOTES

Podcast Rating

Podcast name

....

EPISODE #

RECORDING DATE

PUBLISHING DATE

RECORDING LOCATION

TOPIC TO DISCUSS

....
....
....
....
....
....
....

HOSTS

GUESTS

LENGTH

MAIN GOAL FOR THIS PODCAST

....
....
....
....

CONTEST

SPONSOR ....
PRIZE ....
WINNER ....

TALKING POINTS

....
....
....
....
....
....

Podcast Review

THINGS I NEED TO PRACTICE

THINGS I REALLY ENJOYED :)

THINGS I DIDN'T EXPECTED

BUSINESS / PROMOTION

NOTES

Podcast Rating

Podcast name

....

EPISODE #

RECORDING DATE

PUBLISHING DATE

RECORDING LOCATION

TOPIC TO DISCUSS

....
....
....
....
....
....
....

HOSTS

GUESTS

LENGTH

MAIN GOAL FOR THIS PODCAST

....
....
....
....

CONTEST

SPONSOR ....
PRIZE ....
WINNER ....

TALKING POINTS

....
....
....
....
....
....

Podcast Review

THINGS I NEED TO PRACTICE

THINGS I REALLY ENJOYED :)

THINGS I DIDN'T EXPECTED

BUSINESS / PROMOTION

NOTES

Podcast Rating

Podcast name

....

EPISODE #

RECORDING DATE

PUBLISHING DATE

RECORDING LOCATION

TOPIC TO DISCUSS

....
....
....
....
....
....
....

HOSTS	GUESTS	LENGTH

MAIN GOAL FOR THIS PODCAST

....
....
....
....

CONTEST

SPONSOR ....
PRIZE ....
WINNER ....

TALKING POINTS

....
....
....
....
....
....

Podcast Review

THINGS I NEED TO PRACTICE

....
....
....
....

THINGS I REALLY ENJOYED :)

....
....
....
....

THINGS I DIDN'T EXPECTED

....
....
....
....

BUSINESS / PROMOTION

....
....
....
....
....
....

NOTES

....
....
....
....
....
....

Podcast Rating

Podcast name

....

EPISODE

RECORDING DATE

PUBLISHING DATE

RECORDING LOCATION

TOPIC TO DISCUSS

....
....
....
....
....
....
....

HOSTS

GUESTS

LENGTH

MAIN GOAL FOR THIS PODCAST

....
....
....
....

CONTEST

SPONSOR ....

PRIZE ....

WINNER ....

TALKING POINTS

....
....
....
....
....
....

Podcast Review

THINGS I NEED TO PRACTICE

....
....
....
....

THINGS I REALLY ENJOYED :)

....
....
....
....

THINGS I DIDN'T EXPECTED

....
....
....
....

BUSINESS / PROMOTION

....
....
....
....
....
....

NOTES

....
....
....
....
....
....

Podcast Rating

Podcast name

....

EPISODE #

RECORDING DATE

PUBLISHING DATE

RECORDING LOCATION

TOPIC TO DISCUSS

....
....
....
....
....
....
....

HOSTS	GUESTS	LENGTH

MAIN GOAL FOR THIS PODCAST

....
....
....
....

CONTEST

SPONSOR ....
PRIZE ....
WINNER ....

TALKING POINTS

....
....
....
....
....
....

Podcast Review

THINGS I NEED TO PRACTICE

....
....
....
....

THINGS I REALLY ENJOYED :)

....
....
....
....

THINGS I DIDN'T EXPECTED

....
....
....
....

BUSINESS / PROMOTION

....
....
....
....
....

NOTES

....
....
....
....
....
....

Podcast Rating

Podcast name

....

EPISODE #

RECORDING DATE

PUBLISHING DATE

RECORDING LOCATION

TOPIC TO DISCUSS

....
....
....
....
....
....
....

HOSTS

GUESTS

LENGTH

MAIN GOAL FOR THIS PODCAST

....
....
....
....

CONTEST

SPONSOR ....
PRIZE ....
WINNER ....

TALKING POINTS

....
....
....
....
....
....

Podcast Review

THINGS I NEED TO PRACTICE

....
....
....
....

THINGS I REALLY ENJOYED :)

....
....
....
....

THINGS I DIDN'T EXPECTED

....
....
....
....

BUSINESS / PROMOTION

....
....
....
....
....
....

NOTES

....
....
....
....
....
....

Podcast Rating

Podcast name

....

EPISODE

RECORDING DATE

PUBLISHING DATE

RECORDING LOCATION

TOPIC TO DISCUSS

....
....
....
....
....
....
....

HOSTS

GUESTS

LENGTH

MAIN GOAL FOR THIS PODCAST

....
....
....
....

CONTEST

SPONSOR ....
PRIZE ....
WINNER ....

TALKING POINTS

....
....
....
....
....
....

Podcast Review

THINGS I NEED TO PRACTICE

....
....
....
....

THINGS I REALLY ENJOYED :)

....
....
....
....

THINGS I DIDN'T EXPECTED

....
....
....
....

BUSINESS / PROMOTION

....
....
....
....
....
....

NOTES

....
....
....
....
....

Podcast Rating ☆ ☆ ☆ ☆ ☆

Podcast name

....

EPISODE #

RECORDING DATE

PUBLISHING DATE

RECORDING LOCATION

TOPIC TO DISCUSS

....
....
....
....
....
....
....

HOSTS

GUESTS

LENGTH

MAIN GOAL FOR THIS PODCAST

....
....
....
....

CONTEST

SPONSOR ....
PRIZE ....
WINNER ....

TALKING POINTS

....
....
....
....
....
....

Podcast Review

THINGS I NEED TO PRACTICE

....
....
....
....

THINGS I REALLY ENJOYED :)

....
....
....
....

THINGS I DIDN'T EXPECTED

....
....
....
....

BUSINESS / PROMOTION

....
....
....
....
....

NOTES

....
....
....
....
....

Podcast Rating

Podcast name

....

EPISODE #

RECORDING DATE

PUBLISHING DATE

RECORDING LOCATION

TOPIC TO DISCUSS

....
....
....
....
....
....
....

HOSTS

GUESTS

LENGTH

MAIN GOAL FOR THIS PODCAST

....
....
....
....

CONTEST

SPONSOR ....
PRIZE ....
WINNER ....

TALKING POINTS

....
....
....
....
....
....

Podcast Review

THINGS I NEED TO PRACTICE

THINGS I REALLY ENJOYED :)

THINGS I DIDN'T EXPECTED

BUSINESS / PROMOTION

NOTES

Podcast Rating

Podcast name

....

EPISODE #

RECORDING DATE

PUBLISHING DATE

RECORDING LOCATION

TOPIC TO DISCUSS

....
....
....
....
....
....

HOSTS

GUESTS

LENGTH

MAIN GOAL FOR THIS PODCAST

....
....
....
....

CONTEST

SPONSOR ....
PRIZE ....
WINNER ....

TALKING POINTS

....
....
....
....
....
....

Podcast Review

....
....
....
....

THINGS I REALLY ENJOYED :)

....
....
....
....

THINGS I DIDN'T EXPECTED

....
....
....
....

BUSINESS / PROMOTION

....
....
....
....
....

NOTES

....
....
....
....
....

Podcast Rating

Podcast name

....

EPISODE #

RECORDING DATE

PUBLISHING DATE

RECORDING LOCATION

TOPIC TO DISCUSS

....
....
....
....
....
....
....

HOSTS	GUESTS	LENGTH

MAIN GOAL FOR THIS PODCAST

....
....
....
....

CONTEST

SPONSOR ....
PRIZE ....
WINNER ....

TALKING POINTS

....
....
....
....
....
....

Podcast Review

THINGS I NEED TO PRACTICE

THINGS I REALLY ENJOYED :)

THINGS I DIDN'T EXPECTED

BUSINESS / PROMOTION

NOTES

Podcast Rating

Podcast name

....

EPISODE #

RECORDING DATE

PUBLISHING DATE

RECORDING LOCATION

TOPIC TO DISCUSS

....
....
....
....
....
....
....

HOSTS	GUESTS	LENGTH

MAIN GOAL FOR THIS PODCAST

....
....
....
....

CONTEST

SPONSOR ....
PRIZE ....
WINNER ....

TALKING POINTS

....
....
....
....
....
....

Podcast Review

THINGS I NEED TO PRACTICE

....
....
....
....

THINGS I REALLY ENJOYED :)

....
....
....
....

THINGS I DIDN'T EXPECTED

....
....
....
....

BUSINESS / PROMOTION

....
....
....
....
....

NOTES

....
....
....
....
....
....

Podcast Rating

Podcast name

....

EPISODE #

RECORDING DATE

PUBLISHING DATE

RECORDING LOCATION

TOPIC TO DISCUSS

....
....
....
....
....
....
....

HOSTS	GUESTS	LENGTH

MAIN GOAL FOR THIS PODCAST

....
....
....
....

CONTEST

SPONSOR ....
PRIZE ....
WINNER ....

TALKING POINTS

....
....
....
....
....
....

Podcast Review

THINGS I NEED TO PRACTICE

....
....
....
....

THINGS I REALLY ENJOYED :)

....
....
....
....

THINGS I DIDN'T EXPECTED

....
....
....
....

BUSINESS / PROMOTION

....
....
....
....
....
....

NOTES

....
....
....
....
....
....

Podcast Rating ⭐ ⭐ ⭐ ⭐ ⭐

Podcast name

EPISODE #

RECORDING DATE

PUBLISHING DATE

RECORDING LOCATION

TOPIC TO DISCUSS

HOSTS

GUESTS

LENGTH

MAIN GOAL FOR THIS PODCAST

CONTEST

SPONSOR

PRIZE

WINNER

TALKING POINTS

Podcast Review

THINGS I NEED TO PRACTICE

....
....
....
....

THINGS I REALLY ENJOYED :)

....
....
....
....

THINGS I DIDN'T EXPECTED

....
....
....
....

BUSINESS / PROMOTION

....
....
....
....
....

NOTES

....
....
....
....
....
....

Podcast Rating

Podcast name

....

EPISODE #

RECORDING DATE

PUBLISHING DATE

RECORDING LOCATION

TOPIC TO DISCUSS

....
....
....
....
....
....
....

HOSTS

GUESTS

LENGTH

MAIN GOAL FOR THIS PODCAST

....
....
....
....

CONTEST

SPONSOR ....
PRIZE ....
WINNER ....

TALKING POINTS

....
....
....
....
....
....

Podcast Review

THINGS I NEED TO PRACTICE

THINGS I REALLY ENJOYED :)

THINGS I DIDN'T EXPECTED

BUSINESS / PROMOTION

NOTES

Podcast Rating

Podcast name

....

EPISODE #

RECORDING DATE

PUBLISHING DATE

RECORDING LOCATION

TOPIC TO DISCUSS

....
....
....
....
....
....
....

HOSTS

GUESTS

LENGTH

MAIN GOAL FOR THIS PODCAST

....
....
....
....

CONTEST

SPONSOR ....
PRIZE ....
WINNER ....

TALKING POINTS

....
....
....
....
....
....

Podcast Review

THINGS I NEED TO PRACTICE

....
....
....
....

THINGS I REALLY ENJOYED :)

....
....
....
....

THINGS I DIDN'T EXPECTED

....
....
....
....

BUSINESS / PROMOTION

....
....
....
....
....

NOTES

....
....
....
....
....

Podcast Rating ☆ ☆ ☆ ☆ ☆

Podcast name

EPISODE #

RECORDING DATE

PUBLISHING DATE

RECORDING LOCATION

TOPIC TO DISCUSS

HOSTS

GUESTS

LENGTH

MAIN GOAL FOR THIS PODCAST

CONTEST

SPONSOR

PRIZE

WINNER

TALKING POINTS

Podcast Review

THINGS I NEED TO PRACTICE

THINGS I REALLY ENJOYED :)

THINGS I DIDN'T EXPECTED

BUSINESS / PROMOTION

NOTES

Podcast Rating

Podcast name

EPISODE

RECORDING DATE

PUBLISHING DATE

RECORDING LOCATION

TOPIC TO DISCUSS

HOSTS

GUESTS

LENGTH

MAIN GOAL FOR THIS PODCAST

CONTEST

SPONSOR ....
PRIZE ....
WINNER ....

TALKING POINTS

Podcast Review

THINGS I NEED TO PRACTICE

....
....
....
....

THINGS I REALLY ENJOYED :)

....
....
....
....

THINGS I DIDN'T EXPECTED

....
....
....
....

BUSINESS / PROMOTION

....
....
....
....
....
....

NOTES

....
....
....
....
....

Podcast Rating

Podcast name

....

EPISODE #

RECORDING DATE

PUBLISHING DATE

RECORDING LOCATION

TOPIC TO DISCUSS

....
....
....
....
....
....

HOSTS	GUESTS	LENGTH

MAIN GOAL FOR THIS PODCAST

....
....
....
....

CONTEST

SPONSOR ....
PRIZE ....
WINNER ....

TALKING POINTS

....
....
....
....
....

Podcast Review

THINGS I NEED TO PRACTICE

THINGS I REALLY ENJOYED :)

THINGS I DIDN'T EXPECTED

BUSINESS / PROMOTION

NOTES

Podcast Rating

Podcast name

EPISODE #

RECORDING DATE

PUBLISHING DATE

RECORDING LOCATION

TOPIC TO DISCUSS

....
....
....
....
....
....

HOSTS

GUESTS

LENGTH

MAIN GOAL FOR THIS PODCAST

....
....
....
....

CONTEST

SPONSOR ....

PRIZE ....

WINNER ....

TALKING POINTS

....
....
....
....
....
....

Podcast Review

THINGS I NEED TO PRACTICE

....
....
....
....

THINGS I REALLY ENJOYED :)

....
....
....
....

THINGS I DIDN'T EXPECTED

....
....
....
....

BUSINESS / PROMOTION

....
....
....
....
....
....
....

NOTES

....
....
....
....
....

Podcast Rating

Podcast name

....

EPISODE

RECORDING DATE

PUBLISHING DATE

RECORDING LOCATION

TOPIC TO DISCUSS

....
....
....
....
....
....

HOSTS

GUESTS

LENGTH

MAIN GOAL FOR THIS PODCAST

....
....
....
....

CONTEST

SPONSOR ....

PRIZE ....

WINNER ....

TALKING POINTS

....
....
....
....
....
....

Podcast Review

THINGS I NEED TO PRACTICE

....
....
....
....

THINGS I REALLY ENJOYED :)

....
....
....
....

THINGS I DIDN'T EXPECTED

....
....
....
....

BUSINESS / PROMOTION

....
....
....
....
....
....

NOTES

....
....
....
....
....
....

Podcast Rating

Podcast name

....

EPISODE #

RECORDING DATE

PUBLISHING DATE

RECORDING LOCATION

TOPIC TO DISCUSS

....
....
....
....
....
....
....

HOSTS	GUESTS	LENGTH

MAIN GOAL FOR THIS PODCAST

....
....
....
....

CONTEST

SPONSOR ....
PRIZE ....
WINNER ....

TALKING POINTS

....
....
....
....
....
....

Podcast Review

THINGS I NEED TO PRACTICE

....
....
....
....

THINGS I REALLY ENJOYED :)

....
....
....
....

THINGS I DIDN'T EXPECTED

....
....
....
....

BUSINESS / PROMOTION

....
....
....
....
....
....

NOTES

....
....
....
....
....

Podcast Rating ☆ ☆ ☆ ☆ ☆

Made in United States
North Haven, CT
02 March 2023